CONNECTICUT

Karen Durrie

LET'S READ

AV²
BY WEIGL™

ADDED VALUE • AUDIO VISUAL

AV² provides enriched content that supplements and complements this book. Weigl's AV² books strive to create inspired learning and engage young minds in a total learning experience.

Your AV² Media Enhanced books come alive with...

Audio
Listen to sections of the book read aloud.

Key Words
Study vocabulary, and complete a matching word activity.

Video
Watch informative video clips.

Quizzes
Test your knowledge.

Embedded Weblinks
Gain additional information for research.

Slide Show
View images and captions, and prepare a presentation.

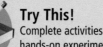

Try This!
Complete activities and hands-on experiments.

... and much, much more!

Go to **www.av2books.com**, and enter this book's unique code.

BOOK CODE

K491434

AV² by Weigl brings you media enhanced books that support active learning.

Published by AV² by Weigl
350 5ᵗʰ Avenue, 59ᵗʰ Floor
New York, NY 10118
Website: www.av2books.com   www.weigl.com

Library of Congress Cataloging-in-Publication Data

Durrie, Karen.
 Connecticut / Karen Durrie.
   p. cm. -- (Explore the U.S.A.)
 Includes bibliographical references and index.
 ISBN 978-1-61913-333-4 (hard cover : alk. paper)
 1. Connecticut--Juvenile literature. I. Title.
 F94.3.D87 2012
 974.6--dc23
                        2012014758

Printed in the United States of America in North Mankato, Minnesota
1 2 3 4 5 6 7 8 9 16 15 14 13 12

052012
WEP040512

Project Coordinator: Karen Durrie
Art Director: Terry Paulhus

Weigl acknowledges Getty Images as the primary image supplier for this title.

CONNECTICUT

Contents

3

This is Connecticut.
It is called the Constitution State.
A constitution is a set of rules
for a country.

This is the shape
of Connecticut.
It is in the east part
of the United States.
Connecticut is one
of the smallest states.

Where is Connecticut?

N
W · E
S

Canada

United States

Pacific
Ocean

Atlantic
Ocean

Mexico

Connecticut is next to
three states.

Settlers came from Europe to Connecticut about 400 years ago. The settlers met American Indians who were living there.

The settlers bought land from the American Indians.

The state flower of Connecticut is the mountain laurel. Mountain laurel bushes can grow up to 18 feet tall.

The state seal has a blue ribbon and three grapevines.

The grapevines stand for the places where people first settled.

This is the state flag of Connecticut. It is blue, white, and gold. The flag has a crest in the middle.

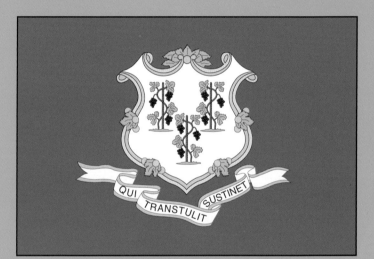

The state motto is shown below the crest.

The state animal of Connecticut is the sperm whale. Sperm whales can grow up to 60 feet long.

Sperm whales have the largest brain of any animal on Earth.

This is the capital city of Connecticut. It is named Hartford. This city has the oldest state house in the United States.

The Old State House in Hartford is more than 215 years old.

Oysters are farmed in Connecticut. Oysters are a kind of shellfish. Pearls sometimes grow inside oysters.

Very few oysters have a perfect pearl inside.

Connecticut has many museums and aquariums.

People from all over the world visit to learn about history and to see many kinds of ocean life.

CONNECTICUT FACTS

These pages provide detailed information that expands on the interesting facts found in the book. These pages are intended to be used by adults as a learning support to help young readers round out their knowledge of each state in the *Explore the U.S.A.* series.

Pages 4–5

Connecticut is called the Constitution State. In the 19th century, Connecticut historian John Fiske claimed that the Fundamental Orders of Connecticut, written between 1638 and 1639, were the first written constitution. Historians believe this document formed the basis for the U.S. Constitution, which was adopted in 1787.

Pages 6–7

On January 9, 1788, Connecticut became the fifth state to join the United States. Connecticut shares borders with Massachusetts, Rhode Island, and New York. The part of the state that borders the Atlantic Ocean touches the Long Island Sound. Connecticut is the third-smallest state, covering an area of 5,544 square miles (14,359 square kilometers).

Pages 8–9

Dutch traders first sailed up the Connecticut River in 1614. They later bought land from the Pequot American Indians to make a permanent settlement. In 1636, Connecticut was one of the first places in North America colonized by Great Britain. Reverend Thomas Hooker, John Haynes, and Roger Ludlow created the town of Hartford and worked to create a new government.

Pages 10–11

Connecticut had a colonial seal that was designed when it was still a British colony. After the Revolutionary War ended in 1783, the seal was altered to better represent the newly formed state. The seal is surrounded by the Latin words *Sigillum reipulicae Connecticutensis*, meaning "the Seal of the State of Connecticut." The seal was adopted in 1784.

KEY WORDS

Research has shown that as much as 65 percent of all written material published in English is made up of 300 words. These 300 words cannot be taught using pictures or learned by sounding them out. They must be recognized by sight. This book contains 64 common sight words to help young readers improve their reading fluency and comprehension. This book also teaches young readers several important content words, such as proper nouns. These words are paired with pictures to aid in learning and improve understanding.

Page	Sight Words First Appearance
5	a, country, for, is, it, of, set, state, the, this
7	in, next, one, part, three, to, where
8	about, American, came, from, Indians, land, there, were, who, years
11	and, can, feet, first, grow, has, mountain, places, up
12	below, white
15	animal, any, Earth, have, long, on
16	city, house, more, named, old, than
19	are, few, kind, live, sometimes, very
20	all, learn, life, many, over, people, see, world

Page	Content Words First Appearance
5	Connecticut, Constitution, rules
7	shape, United States
8	Europe, settlers
11	bushes, flower, grapevines, laurel, ribbon, seal
12	crest, flag, middle, motto
15	brain, sperm whale
16	Hartford, Old State House
19	oysters, pearls, shellfish
20	aquarium, history, museums